BOF! France
funny-side up

Anneke Elwes

Illustrations by Luke Elwes

First published 2007 by Lulu Publishing
www.lulu.com

ISBN 978-0-9556813-0-1

Copyright © 2008 Annke Elwes

The moral rights of the author and illustrator have been asserted.

Typeset by Toja'rt

This book is sold subject to the condition that it shall not, by way of trade or otherwise, be lent, re-sold, hired out, or otherwise circulated without the publisher's prior consent in any form of binding or cover other than that in which it is published and without a similar condition including this condition being imposed on the subsequent purchaser.

*I have tried to lift France out of the mud.
But she will return to her errors and vomitings.
I cannot prevent the French from being French.*

Charles de Gaulle - Former President of France

Contents

Chapter 1 – *Non!* (No way!) 9
Finger Wagging French

Chapter 2 – *Quoi?* (You what?) 17
Lost in Translation

Chapter 3 – *Bof!* (*!?**!) 29
Body Language

Chapter 4 – *Badaboum!* (Crash, bang!) 37
Road Rage

Chapter 5 – *Quel ***!* (You ****!) 47
Gallic Insults

Chapter 6 – *Chou-chou!* (Sweetiepie) 57
Cute bits & Rude bits

Chapter 7 – *Blague!* (Joke!) 67
What the French find Funny

Chapter 8 – *A donf!* (Trendy!) 77
French Fashionistas

Chapter 9 – *Pouah!* (Pooh what a stink!) 95
Lavatorial French

Chapter 10 – *Miam, miam!* (Yum, yum!) 107
Foody French

Chapter 11 – *Bouffe!* (Grub!) 117
Table Manners

Chapter 12 – *Tchin tchin!* (Cheers!)..............................129
Grape Talk

Chapter 13 – *Tchao!* (Hi!) 139
Saying Hello

Chapter 14 – *Puce!* (Flea!) 151
Kids Speak

Chapter 15 – *Ouah! Ouah!* (Woof! Woof!)................... 161
Animal Talk

Chapter 16 – *Branché!* (Cool!) 171
Plugged in French

Chapter 17 – *Ouais!* (YessSSS!).....................................189
Sporting Lingo

La Fin.. 203
The End

Non! (No Way!)
Finger Wagging French

Chapter 1

CHAPTER ONE

Non! (No Way!)

NON! IS PROBABLY THE MOST popular word in the French vocabulary. The French simply love saying *Non! Non! NON!*. Use your nose, lips and throat to spit it out something like GNAW!

Stroppy French people who like to say *Non!* include most officials, waiters and many shopkeepers. Don't take it personally, they treat everyone this way. Of course if you're visiting in August it is even worse, they're working, it's hot and everyone else is on holiday.

IT IS NOT UNUSUAL for the French just to say *non!* and then consider the question. Constantly contradicting and interrupting isn't rude in France; in fact, it's a sign that you're listening and interested. As Dr Johnson, the famous English 18th century writer said:

'*A Frenchman must always be talking whether he knows anything of the matter or not*'

THE FRENCH GOVERNMENT and councils particularly love to wag their finger and say *non!* and if you don't like it you go on strike which is the collective way of finger wagging and saying *non!* back. There's usually a national *non!* campaign about something or other going on somewhere or other.

Striking is a national hobby – they call themselves *râleurs* (whingers) and love an excuse for a public whinge. They'll shout *à bas!* which means 'down with' anything and everything they don't like. Seeing the French protesting and gesticulating *en masse* (altogether) is not only colourful but smelly too – blocking the road with rotting fish or throwing dead sheep at policemen. And its not just the farmers who strike. In 1998 school kids went on strike, when 60,000 of them took to the street. Why? well, rumour has it they wanted to work harder!

Ne Pas Pisser dans la Fontaine

F RANCE IS FULL OF DELIGHTFUL rules which you'll see the French cheerfully ignoring. Here are some typical finger wagging, get lost, don't even think about it *non! Non!*

NON! signs to look out for:

PASSAGE INTERDIT or ENTRÉE INTERDITE No Entry

SORTIE INTERDITE No Exit

STATIONNEMENT INTERDIT No Parking

BAIGNER INTERDIT No bathing

DEFENSE DE FUMER No smoking

NE PAS SE PENCHER Do not lean out

NE PAS TOUCHER Do not touch

DÉFENSE D'ENTRER Keep Out

DÉFENSE DE LAVER LA VAISELLE DANS LES LAVABOS –
No washing up in the basins (a favourite in campsites)

INTERDIT AUX MOINS DE 13 ANS – *Under 13s not allowed*

DÉFENSE DE NOURRIR LES ANIMAUX
– Don't feed the animals

DÉFENSE DE TOUCHER – *Don't touch*

DÉFENSE DE MARCHER SUR LA PELOUSE – *Keep off the grass*

CHIEN MECHANT – *Beware of the dog*

Quoi? (You what?!)
Lost in Translation

CHAPTER TWO
Quoi? (You what?!)

THE FRENCH ARE FOREIGN and most don't (or won't) speak English. Even worse, they think you're the foreigner and pity you for not being French. The French you learn from books they pretend they can't understand at all. And there's nothing new about this.

'In Paris they simply stared when I spoke to them in French. I never did succeed in making those idiots understand their language'
(Mark Twain, American writer 1835-1910)

THE NEXT PROBLEM IS THAT the French don't sound like us. They may be a noisy lot but they make very different noises. Speaking French is a bit like trying to talk when you've got a really bad cold. The vowels are nasal. Try saying *un bon vin blanc* (a good white wine) over and over. Try it again as if you've got a blocked nose. See what I mean? It's a lot easier to do if you're young and have a mobile tongue and lips, the older you are the harder the pronunciation.

Try these out:

Oui! : not so much *wee* as **Oo ee!**	– yes!
Non! : not so much *noh* as **Gnaw!**	– no!
S'il vous plaît : **Seelvooplay**	– please
Au revoir : **Orvwar**	– bye
Excusez-moi : **Exkewzay-mwah**	– excuse me
Porquoi?: **Poorkwah?**	– why?
Parlez vous Anglais? : **Parlay-voo ong-glay**	– Speak English?
Je ne comprends pas : **Jer ner comprong pah**	– don't understand

Puis-je l'essayer? : **Pweej lessayay?** – Can I try it on?

Où sont les toilettes? : **Oo song lay twullett?** – Where's the loo?

L'addition s'il vous plaît : **Ladeesseeong seelvooplay** – bill please

A few tips on sounds:

an and *en* are best said as if someone's just punched you in the chest

ain is said as if you're having your tonsils inspected

'*r*' is vibrated like you're trying to clear your throat

'*u*' is the worst – rather like trying to make the sound of a whistling kettle

YOU CAN ALWAYS GET YOUR own back with 'h' which the French just can't say and 'w' which isn't really a French letter at all (look in a French dictionary and you'll find most of the words beginning in 'w' are *franglais*). They definitely do drop their aitches though, they just can't help it. So after a hard day of trying to speak the lingo you can have a laugh at their expense and get them to try to say house not 'ouse or Homer not 'Omer or happy not 'appy or here not 'ere!

The bad news is that French is not written as it is pronounced and as most French people can't write a letter without spelling mistakes, we don't stand much of a chance. But the good news is that you can ignore a lot of written French. If you see an 'h' – just ignore it. And if you see a plural 's' at the end of a French word – ignore it! And if you see consonants at the end of words – ignore them!

Historical Note
The Académie Française was created 400 years ago to unify the various French dialects into one common language.

And the even better news is that English is catching on, fast. If it carries on at this rate there won't be much French left to learn. The French are desperately trying to hold back this tide of English (or 'Disney-speak' as they call it). They even disguise Hollywood blockbusters. First they dub them into French wherever possible and then they change the film's name – so 'Jaws', for example, became *Les Dents de la Mer* (The Teeth of the Sea).

THE *ACADÉMIE FRANÇAISE* IS responsible for keeping the French language pure. It is run by 40 people in the centre of Paris – mostly doddery, ancient bookworms who are known as *les immortels* (the immortals). Their job is to edit the encyclopaedia that determines what is acceptable French. They believe French should remain as French as possible but since new words often come from other languages, this poses a bit of a problem. It might be 'pure French' on paper but it's not very

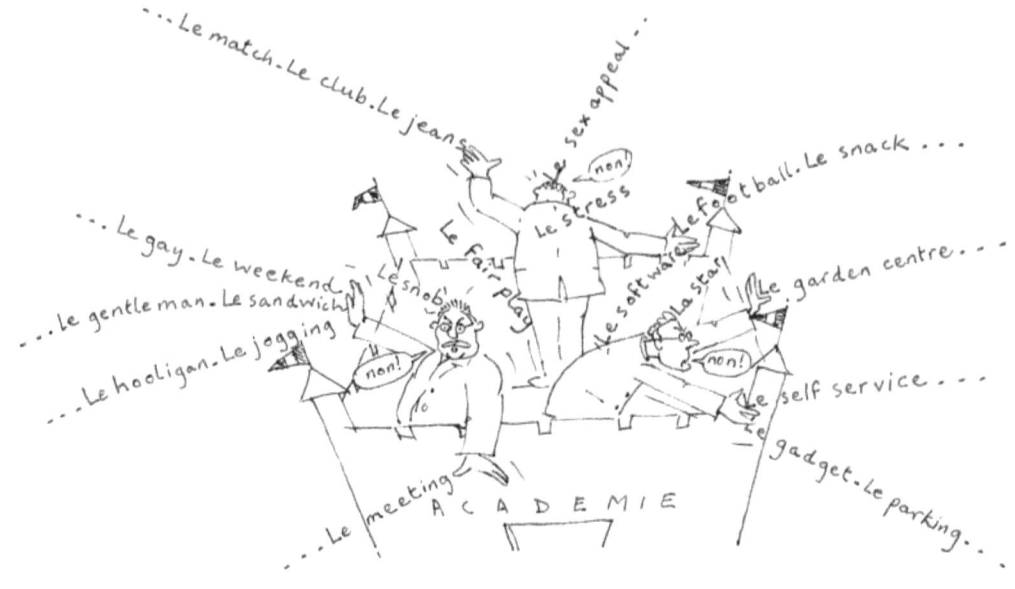

pure out there on the street. French slang does get included after a time lag because the French take great pride in its creativity, but much of the French in this book hasn't got there yet (but they'll get there in time – after all it took them 350 years to elect a woman to the *Académie*). *Les immortels* haven't dared to update the great encyclopaedia since 1994. What they are really scratching their heads over is how to come up with new French technology words to keep English terms like email, software and blog out of the French language. The problem is the English words are short and catchy and the words *les immortels* come up with are usually twice as long and unpronounceable (even to the French). Ah well, if they weren't so immortal it would be someone else's problem by now.

HOWEVER MUCH *FRANGLAIS* enters the French language, the French will never adopt the English habit of understatement. Where we might describe something as 'great', the French have a whole language of superlatives and hand gestures to go with them to show just how impressed they really are.

Super! (super!)
Trop fort! (it's too strong – ie. it's wicked)
Géant! (It's giant!)
C'est magnifique! (magnificent!)
C'etait formidable! (formidable!)

And they love to stress every syllable like a strong rhythm that builds to a crescendo with the last syllable *c'est <u>mag</u>-<u>ni</u>-<u>fique!</u>* or *c'est <u>for</u>-<u>mid</u>-<u>able !</u>* or, to express disbelief *c'est <u>in</u>-<u>ad</u>-<u>miss-ible!</u>* (it's not possible!) and *c'est <u>rid</u>-<u>i</u>-<u>cule!</u>* (it's outrageous!)

And don't forget, French hands are never still so take yours out of your pockets and put them to work.

Bof! (*!?**!)
Body Language

Chapter 3

CHAPTER THREE
Bof! (*!?**!)

IF YOU'RE STILL HAVING trouble being understood, let your body do the talking instead.

The French have perfected the art of body language. They believe bottling up your feelings is bad for you, so they have developed a colourful language to let you know exactly what they think. And it really is a language all of its own. Their looks, shrugs and gestures say it all.

- The shrug that says *you pathetic idiot!* (they do this one very well)
- The gesture which says *I don't give a damn!* (this is a good one for getting what you want in France)
- The look that says *how can you come out dressed like that?*

THE FRENCH ARE IMPATIENT and quickly bored. They don't believe in smiling and nodding politely. In fact if you smile too much they think you're stupid. So don't bother to make people like you or win them over, just play them at their own game.

Here are a few must-know gestures definitely worth practising.

Elementary level – but getting ruder...

MEANS I don't know / I don't really want to know / that's not on

Raise eyebrows and do a surrender sign at shoulder height

MEANS you've had enough – I've had it up to here.

Mark an imaginary line across the forehead with the righ hand, palm down.

Complètement cinglé

MEANS totally crazy.

Tap your index finger on the side of the head and say: *complètement cinglé!*

mon oeil !

MEANS 'oh yeah?' 'think I was born yesterday?' or 'pull the other one'. Where we might say 'my foot!', they say 'my eye!'

To do this pull down the skin under the right eye with the right index finger.

Quelle barbe !

MEANS I'm fed up / you're boring. For some strange reason this comes from shaving. *Barbant* or *rasant* which mean boredom come from barber and *rasoir* (to shave). What a bore is what a beard!

So if you're irritated with someone and want to indicate that they're a bore, rub your cheek with the back of your hand – as if feeling how smooth a shave is. Anyone can do this whether they've got a hairy cheek or not.

> MEANS you're drunk or completely pissed.
>
> **Turn your right hand in front of your nose and say:** *complètement bourré!*

Complètement bourré!

Advanced level

Definitely rude and only to be used under extreme provocation

The Paris shrug (which goes on all over France it's just that they are particularly good at it in Paris). It is the ultimate gesture of complete and utter indifference to you, your plight and your existence on this planet. **How to spot it:** shoulders, arms and ribcage take off vertically, accompanied often by the sound *'Bof!'* (pronounced more like beuphf!) which is pretty untranslatable but means something along the lines of 'I don't give a toss!'

But the supreme gesture and overall winner in the rudeness stakes is, without doubt, *le bras d'honneur.* It is rather grandly called the gesture of respect, but it is in fact the complete opposite, it is the French equivalent of the V-sign or giving someone the finger and means Up yours! Get stuffed! Or **** you! French drivers are renowned for it and of course it involves removing both hands from the steering wheel. Note: it is useful for a passenger in your car to master this one.

Once you start looking you'll see these gestures everywhere, practise them, and you could become as rude as the French.

Badaboum!
(Crash, bang!)
Road Rage

CHAPTER FOUR
Badaboum! *(Crash, bang!)*

NON-FRENCH DRIVERS venturing onto French roads take their life into their hands. Crossroads and stop signs are seen as an insult to French liberty and can interrupt conversations that usually involve the driver facing sideways and often backwards too. In fact all traffic rules are treated as no more than interesting suggestions. Did you know that there's a road accident in France every 5 seconds?

Two basic rules to remember:

1. Red traffic lights rank alongside queues in France and are considered to be only for those with time to waste. They even have a phrase for it – brûler le feu rouge – burn the red light.
2. The appropriate insulting gesture is more important than keeping your hands on the wheel (so learn le b*ras d'honneur*

– see previous chapter: *Bof!*)

The French tend to buy cars for life. They favour small, timid cars not because they intend driving them timidly but because they are cheaper to tax. Small cars in France are especially cheeky and love nothing more than the challenge of overtaking a big powerful car.

The quintessential small French car remains the 2CV. Despite no longer being in production, the French love affair with the 2CV still rages on and because it is so French in character, the French have named it the most intelligent car in the world (of course).

EVERY FRENCH DRIVER 'wants to be the one in front'. They drive fast and only slow down or give way for posses of lurid, lycra-clad racing cyclists for whom they have grudging respect.

𝕳istorical 𝕹ote
The 2CV was designed by Citroen with a suspension that allowed a farmer to drive over a field carrying eggs to market without breaking them.

Here's some important motoring lingo for you to test drive:

▶ Boy racers are *les chauffards* and they typically *coller aux fesses* – drive up your bum.

▶ *Faire une queue de poisson* – to do a fishtail – is to overtake and then cut in close in front of the car you've just overtaken, a French speciality.

▶ *Appuyer sur le champignon* – to press on the mushroom is to step on it – old style accelerators look remarkably like large field mushrooms.

▶ *Rentrer dans le décor* – to enter the scenery is their rather poetic way of describing driving off the road.

THE FRENCH COUNTRYSIDE can appear very empty and uninhabited. And unless it's market day, everyone seems to be asleep in the towns as well. This doesn't stop the French however, from advertising their towns as if the only purpose of French roads is to connect one town of fabulously important cultural and historic significance to the next.

And just so that you know that you're nearly there a mad water tower construction will appear on the horizon.

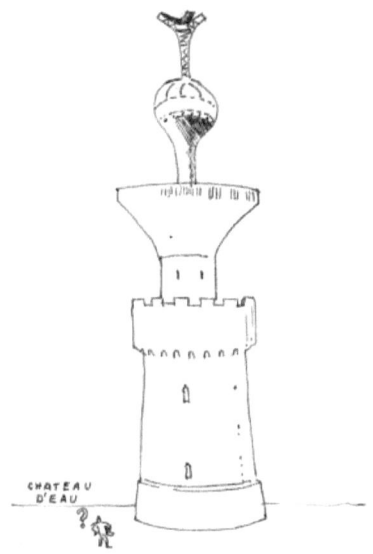

The number on the plate of a French car tells you where it's from. Look out for number plates with either 75 (central Paris) or 78, 91, 92, 93, 94, 95 (Paris suburbs) and then show your contempt for their generally more aggressive driving skills by gesticulating and shouting *'ces sales Parigots'* (Parisian bastards) as you would if you were a Frenchman from anywhere in France other than Paris (a word of warning: don't try this in Paris).

A coach is called *un car* in French so you could confuse your driver by calling out '*un car*' when you overtake a coach.

A few French road signs to look out for:

french driver
after a good lunch

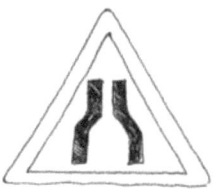
wine bottleneck

sleeping french
police woman

short Emperor ahead

Load, aim, fire!

M * * * *!

*Quel ***!* (You ****!)
Gallic Insults

CHAPTER FIVE

*Quel ***!* (You ****!)

ONCE YOU HAVE MASTERED the actions, you still need to learn how to swear like the French to convince them that you are, in fact, using their language. Swearing is so associated with French that in English we have the phrase *'Pardon my French'* to excuse rude language. In fact the French use all their 4-letter words so regularly in everyday speech that they don't really consider it swearing at all.

Victor Hugo, the great French writer, once called it 'a language of combat' since the French, as you might expect, excel themselves with their range of insults. They have a strong sense of their own superiority and no problem expressing their contempt for people they consider inferior, which is pretty much everyone.

Nicknames

WE MAY CALL THEM 'FROGS' and the Simpsons famously called them 'cheese-eating surrender monkeys' but they call us English *Les rosbifs* (roast beefs because of our taste for overcooked meat), Americans *Ricains* or *Yankees*, Italians *Macaronis* and Germans *Boche* or *Fritz*. It could of course be worse, and for some nationalities it is.

Jean-Paul Sartre, their famous 20th century writer and thinker, summed it up with the immortal words: *L'enfer, c'est les autres* – hell is other people (thanks, Jean-Paul).

L'enfer, c'est les autres

And if those other people are making your life hell then here are some useful ways to tell them to get lost:

Comprend pas	Don't understand
Sais pas	Dunno
J'y vais	Gotta go
Dégage	Get lost
Occupe-toi de tes oignons!	Mind your own onions (business)!
J'en ai assez	I've had enough
Je m'en fous	I don't give a damn
C'est une arnaque!	It's a rip off!
Être sans un radis	Not got a penny (a radish)
Tu commences à me casser!	You are really beginning to piss me off!
Casse-toi!	Beat it!

Insults

And if you annoy the French you may well hear one or more phrases from the following list:

You are...

un abruti – an idiot

un crétin – a twit

un bouffon – a fool

un minus – a dead loss (to someone smaller than you)

But if you really annoy them you might hear some serious insults:

un fumier – a shit (manure)

un batard – a bastard

un salaud – also a bastard

une salope – a bitch

un putain – an arsehole

un chiant – a pain in the arse

un enfoiré – a dickhead

Swear words

SO MUCH FOR INSULTS. Now for swear words that you will never see in a text book: first **con!**

It's a close relation of our 4-letter words and it applies equally well to men and women:

male version – *un con or un connard*
female version – *une conne or une connarde / connasse*

𝔥istorical 𝔑ote

Did you know that the V-sign originated at the Battle of Agincourt in 1415 when the English fought the French? Traditionally English archers captured by the French had the two fingers they used for steadying the arrow chopped off so that they could no longer fight. After their great victory at Agincourt the archers did the V-sign to the remaining French on the battlefield – we've still got our fingers so up yours!

Chapter 5

With *quel con!* you've pretty much got what a *****ing idiot! And there are many variations on the theme including *ducon* which means prick and *tête de con* which means something like wanker. *Faire le con* means to be out of order and *avoir déconné* is to piss about.

The problem with *con!* is that it may be rude but because everyone uses it (including teachers to pupils), it just doesn't sound particularly rude anymore, more like 'you stupid git'. So for a super strength, four star, mega swear word we need to go up a level to: **enculé!**

And if it's a rude verb you're after rather than a noun *foutre* can be handy. Say *va te faire foutre!* and you're pretty close to telling them to ****off!

So there you have it, a foul-mouthed summary for *ta gueule* – (you animal mouth). And if you don't like it, you can *écrase!* or *ferme-la!* (shut up)!

Chou-chou!
(Sweetie pie!)
Cute bits & Rude bits

CHAPTER SIX
Chou-chou! (Sweetie pie!)

HOWEVER DON'T BELIEVE the French are always rude and aggressive. Just as often they are sweet and affectionate. If they like you this is what you might hear:

- *c'est mignon* – is sweeeeet!
- *chou-chou* (which literally means 'cabbage-cabbage') is sweetie pie or teacher's pet
- *mon lapin* (which literally means my rabbit) and is also sweetie pie or bunny.
- *tu es adorable* means you're very cute but best used only for very small children or animals.

- best friends in French are *co-pains comme cochons* – friends like pigs. So next time you see your best friend remember to call them a pig.

And if you want to talk to the opposite sex, learn the lingo. Romantic words:

mon bébé (my baby)

mon chéri (my darling)

mon cœur (my heart)

mon chaton d'amour (my love kitten)

And kisses are *bises*.

IF YOU FEEL YOU'VE REALLY hit it off you could say *nous avons les atomes crochus* – we have hooked atoms – isn't that sweet? As for love at first sight, that's a bolt of lightning in French – *le coup-de-foudre*.

The French don't really have a word for boyfriend or girlfriend. They sometimes say 'a little friend' *un(e) petit(e) ami(e)*.

But there are slang words so if you're cool and streetwise you'd say *ma pépée* for girlfriend (not to be confused with *pipi* which is French for piss) and *mon jules* for boyfriend.

To chat someone up, the French say *faire du plat à quelqu'un* to make dish to somebody. If a boy is cute, you say he's *mignon*. If a girl is a real babe you say *bombe* or *canon* – like a sex bomb, but a sex canon...?

To be sex crazed is *être un chaud lapin* – to be a hot rabbit. The French have always thought of themselves as a race of hot rabbits and in Victorian Britain we thought they were hot rabbits too. So there was channel–hopping for hanky panky and naughty new words like French kiss (that's the one involving tongues) and French letter (condom) and French maid (sexy and fun) entered the language. For the strait-laced Victorians France was a land of pleasure.

> ### Historical Note
> *Many of these terms date back to Napoleonic times when the French called Britain 'Perfide Albion' meaning deceitful Britain and used these insults as a rallying cry for recruiting troops to fight the terrible English.*

THE FRENCH RETURNED the compliment by describing anything that took the fun out of being sexy as 'English'. So a condom is called *une capote anglaise* (an English cap). And homosexuality is *le vice anglais* (the English vice because they thought most Englishmen were gay)

Strangest of all is *avoir ses anglais* or *les Anglais débarquent* (the English have landed) which means a woman's period has started. Apparently this has something to do with the invading redcoats – the English troops who fought Napoleon.

Not surprisingly the French are pretty graphic and don't hold back when it comes to describing how sexy they are.

So, which do you fancy?

▶ *une grande femme poilue, chauve et barbue* (a tall, hairy, bald and bearded woman)

▶ or *un petit homme, bien roule avec des guiboles de rêve et avec une grosse poitrine* (a small, curvy, big-breasted man with great legs)?

And then of course there are all those other bits so here's the slang that goes with them:

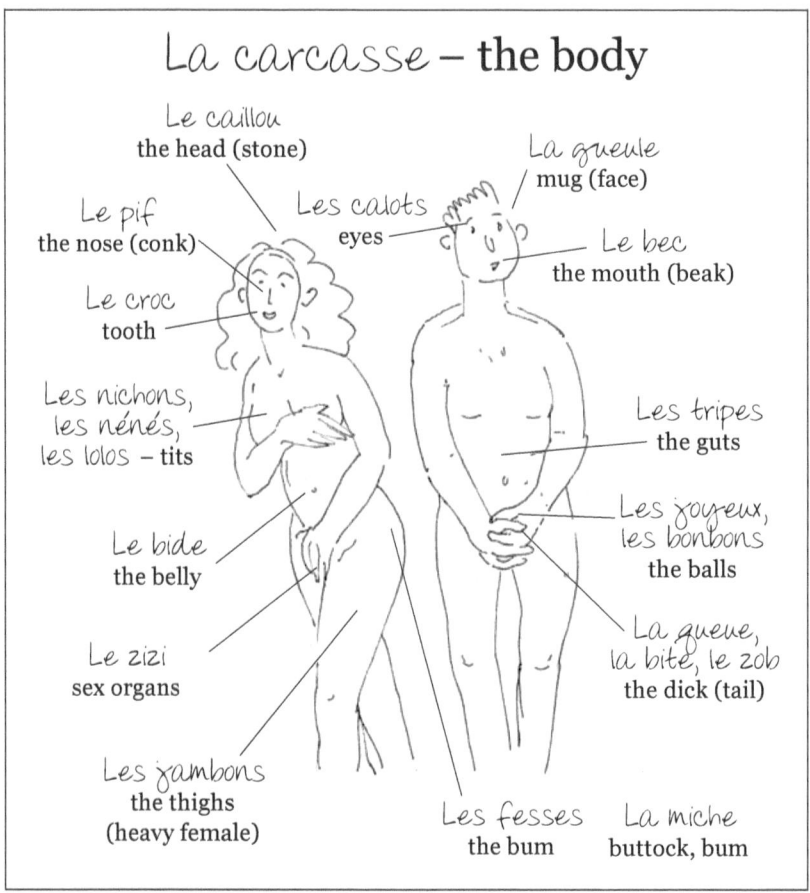

Big boobs in French are *gros roberts, roberts* being the name of a famous brand of baby milk.

But the French don't judge others by their looks.

Well not usually.

Not always.

Only when they need to…..

Because they've just seen a big woman who looks like a large horse *(un grand cheval),* or a fat slob (*un gros lard* – big bacon fat), or someone with too much make-up (*la pot de peinture* – the paint pot) or someone self-important (*une grosse légume* – a big vegetable), or a dumpy woman (*un pot à tabac* – a tobacco pot), or a peasant (*un cul-terreux* – one whose bum is covered in earth) or a bald head (*la boule à zéro* – a zero ball) or a show off (*m'as-tu vu?* – a have you seen me?) or a complete tramp (*un ours mal léché* – a badly licked bear)…

Blague! (Joke!)
What the French find Funny

CHAPTER SEVEN
Blague! (Joke!)

WE KNOW THE FRENCH are good at insults and have a colourful language. But do they have a sense of humour? The French would probably see this as a very English question. In the eighteenth century the French were mystified by this English 'youmor' (this was how they tried to pronounce it). The French had *humeur,* meaning mood, but not 'humour', meaning making people laugh and putting them in a good *humeur.* They had to wait another 150 years before humour joined

English youmor

Historical Note

In 1762 the French writer and philosopher, Voltaire, made this remark about the British and humour: 'they believe that they are the only people who have it'

humeur in the great encyclopaedia of French. Remember, those old bookworms at the *Académie Française* like to take their time, especially when it comes to approving an English word. The French do see 'humour' as particularly English and love all zany, off the wall, English things from Alice in Wonderland to Monty Python, Mr Bean and Absolutely Fabulous.

They laugh at our jokes but do we laugh at theirs? In a recent on line survey, this was the joke the French found the funniest:

An Alsatian went to a telegram office, took out a blank form and wrote: "Woof. Woof. Woof. Woof. Woof. Woof. Woof. Woof. Woof." The clerk examined the paper and politely told the dog: "There are only nine words here. You could send another 'Woof' for the same price." "But," the dog replied, "that would make no sense at all." Weird.

TALKING OF DOGS, the French also love hoaxes (convincing people things are real) and there is a great tradition of telephone hoaxes. One of the best known and best loved is when Jean-Yves Lafesse convinced the French RSPCA that not only was his dog the world trampolining champion, but that it had taken off so sky high, it had never come back to earth.

They also go in for a lot of spoofs – spoof programmes, spoof ads, there is even a spoof band called the *Bratisla Boys* who'll sing any old thing and invariably get it to the top of the French charts – which says a lot about the French pop scene.

THE FRENCH LIKE THE surreal and the farcical (silly pranks). Switch on one of their channels first thing in the morning and you might be accosted by a French comedian who runs around the streets completely stark naked armed only with a megaphone. In fact to be described as 'crazy' by the French can be a compliment – it means they think you're funny (unless it's shouted from another car with the index finger tapping the side of the head, in which case it's best ignored).

The French like to make fun of other people but aren't so keen on making fun of themselves. They don't see the point of talking about their own lives and experiences in order to make others laugh. This is too close to appearing a fool and the French don't suffer fools gladly. However if they think someone else is a fool then that's no problem. Particularly if that person is in a position of power – the 3 P's of power being politicians, police and priests. They love taking the piss out of people who take themselves seriously (and since a lot of people do this in France it's like an endless merry go round). They call this *ridicule* which is the art of making others seem ridiculous.

This can all get pretty nasty as comedians have *carte blanche* (complete freedom) to lay into politicians. Inspired by the English TV series Spitting Image which used puppets to impersonate politicians, the French came up with *Les Guignols* – the same idea but much harder hitting and it has been accused of effecting the outcome of several French elections. French comedians are sometimes seen as resistance fighters or popular philosophers – so maybe they've started to take themselves too seriously and what's needed now is someone to take the piss out of French comedians?

So when they're not arguing the toss, French comedians are conducting a love affair with their own language. They love *le mot juste* (the exact right expression), *les bon mots* (wit) and *jeux des mots* (wordplay). In this sense they are much more in the tradition of Shakespeare than English comedians. They see themselves as poets twisting the language every which way and playing with its rhythms and meaning. Rapid fire jokes and exchanges between French comedians can be like verbal ping pong, full of puns and play on words. No doubt it's all very clever and very funny but we'll have to take their word for it as it's all untranslatable gobbledy-gook and double Dutch for us mere foreign mortals.

> **Historical Note**
> René Goscinny and Albert Uderzo created the most successful cartoon ever with Asterix. It has been translated into 72 languages. They also wrote Lucky Luke.

ONE OF THE BIGGEST challenges has been translating the ever popular *Asterix* (written by a Frenchman in French) and *Tintin* (written by a Belgian in French). Most of the jokes are wordplays, puns or animal noises and depend on the fact that French has so many words that sound the same but mean very different things. The French phrase *double entendre* means exactly this – double hearing or double meanings. The problem is the joke gets lost in the translation. Lots of the sound effects have been kept in French like *flac! aie! boum! ouf!* They just sound right even if they don't mean a thing, especially in Chinese.

We can join in the joke, however, with French visual humour. The French have a great tradition from legendary mime artists like Marcel Marceau, to the body language and absurd scrapes and messes Jacques Tati gets into as Monsieur Hulot, through to classy contemporary circus acts like *Le Cirque de Soleil*.

A Donf! (Trendy!)
French Fashionistas

CHAPTER EIGHT
A Donf! (Trendy!)

So, WHAT'S THE NEW BLACK? as they say in the fashion industry. Will it be white socks? Turbans? Fake pearls? Bubble skirts? Metallic trousers? Real fake fur? Schoolboy shorts on girls? Teenage vampires? Afro puffs (making holes in your baseball cap and pulling your hair through them)? Torn ruffles? Tattoo tributes?

We must wait, with baited breath, for the lords and ladies of the fashion industry to tell us what to wear each year at the January fashion shows (what we must all wear in the spring and summer) and at the July fashion shows (what we must all wear in the autumn and winter).

When the coolest dudes of the French fashion business, Marc Jacob (of the 'Marc' line to be found on all high streets) and Nicolas Ghesquière (the current beautiful boy of fashion) are

> **Historical Note**
> In the past the Fashion Houses took great pleasure in declaring a new skirt length every season so everyone had to change their wardrobe. Just after the miniskirt became popular in the 1970's the Paris collections brought in long skirts. By then the savvy just stuck to trousers.

asked 'what's the new black?' they just give a Paris shrug and sip their (black) coffee. It's hip not to care.

Well, they might pretend not to care, but they'll still fight tooth and nail to dress a Hollywood star who's tipped to win an Oscar or design a royal princess's wedding dress.

Where would they all be without their dolls to dress – the great filmstars of the past: Greta Garbo, Marlene Dietrich, Audrey Hepburn; the Jo-Lo's of now, rockstars like Madonna, Arabian princesses, pampered wives of billionaires and crowned heads of Europe?

Haute Couture (which means high sewing) is the ultimate indulgence for luxury women who will jetset between Paris, London, New York and Milan to get first choice of the most exclusive output of the big fashion houses.

If you've got the dosh then you can meet the maestro and have his or her artistic vision adapted especially for you. The legendary fashion designer, Balenciaga, was known for making the outfits on his clients and improving their figures with a few nips and tucks (ouch!).

Fashionista landing

Ok, so the evening dress might set you back 40,000 pounds but you'll be told you look like a million dollar babe and that no one in the world will have anything similar (but don't you believe it as the paparazzi cameras always manage to find someone else in the same frock). But it will make you a big vegetable – *un grand légume* (bigwig), as the French would say, and buys you VIP treatment at the fashion shows – an invitation not by post but by personal messenger and a front row seat.

To be a top designer in a French fashion house it helps to be a power-crazed, egomaniac who knows how to behave like a superstar. So long as you can outperform your clients you don't even have to be French.

Try it at home.

A BIT OF BAD BEHAVIOUR combined with the twenty year rule and you might be on to something. The twenty year rule works on the basis that sounds and looks repeat themselves every twenty years so to predict the next big music or fashion trend just look at what was around twenty years ago (Addidas did this when they launched the 'old school trainer' look). So:

1. Choose something that was around 20 years ago.
2. Get the cool kids at school wearing it.
3. Make friends with celebrities or blackmail them to be photographed with it.
4. Make sure it's scarce, so limit stock and make subtle changes to keep it exclusive.
5. Get some zombies or aliens to model it.
6. Hire friends to look important by taking notes and talking incessantly on their mobiles
7. Remember to always, always look cool and distant, as if there are loads of places where you'd far rather be.
8. And don't forget the logo and the rip-offs, oops, I mean the spin-offs – ridiculously priced sunglasses, scarves, perfumes, make-up and bags.

It's worked before.

Coco Chanel

GREAT MAESTROS past and present include Christian Dior, Yves St Laurent, John Galliano, Jean-Paul Gaultier, Tom Ford, Karl Lagerfeld, Christian Lacroix and Pierre Cardin.

But it wasn't always dominated by men. Coco Chanel was such a legend that her life has been turned into a musical 'Coco'. She was raised in an orphanage where she learnt to sew. After a brief stint as a cabaret singer (she sang a song called *cocorico* – cock-a-doodle-doo which earned her the nickname Coco) she opened a hat shop. At a time of corsets and hoop skirts she was designing fashion for women inspired by men.

It was her 1926 'little black dress' which made black fashionable. By 1935 Coco had 4,000 workers and smart Americans crossed the Atlantic to attend her shows (lots of black and white, tweed

> **Historical Note**
> *During the war silk was used for parachutes whilst wool and leather was needed for uniforms and boots. As a result cloth for dresses was severely rationed. When the Allies liberated Paris they banned all long designer skirts.*

and gold buttons) and those of her great rival – Elsa Schiaparelli (shocking pink and huge shoulders padded with chicken feathers). But Coco outscored Elsa on colourful lifestyles; she had affairs with English Dukes and Russian royalty and lived in the Hotel Ritz throughout the second world war (although an affair with a Nazi officer led to 10 years exile in Switzerland after the war).

Coco was also responsible for great fashion pronouncements such as: *'simplicity is the keynote of all true elegance'* (OK Coco, we'll buy that).

'fashion is not simply a matter of clothes. Fashion is in the air, born upon the wind…(hang on a second, Coco)…*It is in the sky and on the road…*

But after the war – when big business took over – a man (Jacques Fath) declared that: *'fashion is an art and men are the artists'* (sorry, Coco).

THE FIRST BIG HONCHO after the war was Christian Dior who brought back femininity and glamour and made Paris the centre of world fashion again. Dior caused a scandal at a time of austerity and rationing with extravagant dresses and full blown skirts that needed as much as 27 meters of material. Tut tut Christian!

An interesting offshoot of war time fabric rationing was the bikini. Developed not by a haughty *haute couturier* but by a car engineer called Louis Reard with a sideline in lingerie. To keep things to the bare minimum (literally) he created two small triangles for the top and two bigger triangles for the bottom out of no more than 75cms of fabric. The Americans then came to his aid with a name when they tested nuclear bombs on a group of Pacific islands called the Bikini atoll.

Louis struggled to find anyone respectable to model his new invention so he hired an exotic dancer from the not so respectable Casino de Paris. *Quelle sensation!*

The French loved it although other Catholic countries banned

M. Reard and his creation

bikinis from their beaches and for a long time they were kept out of Hollywood movies for fear of the French and their *chaud lapin* (hot rabbit) raunchy ways. However the bikini finally made it across the Atlantic in the 1960's with beach parties and the song *'Itsy Bitsy Teenie Weenie Yellow Polka Dot Bikini'*.

Yves Saint Laurent

THE GREAT FRENCH fashion designer of the 60's was Yves Saint Laurent or YSL as his label became known. He took over Christian Dior, the most famous fashion house in the world, at the age of 21. He made it acceptable for women to wear trousers. He also loved transparent materials and in 1965 said:

'I think it is more interesting to see the body of a woman when she wears something free, something loose'

This thinking from the great maestro has influenced all Frenchmen since who believe that when it comes to women, the less clothes and the more transparent the clothes, the better.

So you see female flesh used to sell all kinds of products to Frenchmen in French advertising.

A scantily dressed woman on a French billboard has led male drivers to *rentrer dans le décor* (that is, to enter the scenery). Even Marianne, the symbol of *La République* seems to be having trouble keeping her clothes on as she leaps over the barricades.

Since YSL we've had Michelle Rosier, – known as 'vinyl girl' – who had a thing about plastics and metal, André Courrèges who claims he invented the mini-skirt (ask any English person and

they'll tell you it was actually Mary Quant), Jean-Paul Gaultier, the bad punk boy of fashion, who had Madonna strutting on stage in a corset with metal bra cones and Karl Lagerfeld who brought back £10,000 Chanel suits for 1980s power dressing.

BUT NONE OF THIS IS a twentieth century phenomenon. All fashion eyes have been on Paris since the days of Louis XIV who was short and bald and started the male fashion for wigs and high heels. Hair dos were the talk of the town in those days.

> *It was a hairstyle into which one introduced persons or things one liked, such as portraits of one's children or friends, the picture of one's dog, of one's bird, all framed with one's father's or lover's hair.*
> Mme de Oberkirch 1770s

Please yourself Madame, it'll never catch on…

But it did, and there were hairstyles with wire constructions as much as four times the height of a woman's head leading to talk of raising the height of doors. One famous hair do had a built-in ship under full sail to honour a great victory at sea. Apparently ladies of the court were known to sleep in an upright position to preserve their hair do which earned them the gratitude of the mice that often nested inside.

And then there were the cosmetics – pork fat and wax on the

hair, red (crushed beetle) and white paint (lead) for the face....

So Madonna, count yourself lucky that all you had to wear to keep the French fashionistas happy was a rocket-head bra.

Fashion even had a Minister who decreed things such as the length of court dress trains (the bit that drags behind on the floor). It could be 11 feet for the Queen of France, 9 feet for the royal princesses, more distant relations of the king 7 feet, princesses who were not daughters of the king 5 feet, and duchesses 3 feet. When they walked they'd have to loop these trains up over their left arms (not right – never forget the Minister of Fashion might be lurking behind a bush) to keep them out of the mud, the dog poos and from tripping up the rest of the French court.

S O, WHILST PARIS TELLS the world what to wear, what do we wear to Paris? *What to wear in Paris* is a question commonly typed into search engines. And the answer is.... much the same as you'd wear at home. French boys look to the US or the UK for street fashion. You'd be hard pressed to find a French male under the age of 60 in a beret , instead teenagers are happy to slouch around in hoods and *la casquette de baseball à l'envers* – a back to front baseball cap.

As for French girls, it's official, they prefer trousers – *taille basse* – hipsters and heels or *le style Baggy Vans* – baggy trousers with chunky trainers or for a more feminine, sexy, popstar look – *pantalons serrés* – tight trousers with pointy shoes.

General rule when dressing in France is: same as us but a bit sexier, which means better fitted, body hugging clothes and the odd well chosen accessory such as costume jewellery or a scarf. The assumption is that you have a good figure and want to wear clothes to show it off to best effect. A tightly ribbed polo neck jumper can look sexier than a low cleavage. The French believe that the rightful place for minimum clothing / maximum flesh is either the bedroom or the beach. So remember no bum cracks, bouncing boobs or guts hanging out over jeans!

Pouah!
(Pooh what a stink!)
Lavatorial French

CHAPTER NINE

Pouah! (Pooh what a stink!)

Pissing in Public

FIRSTLY THERE'S THE French public loo – you will quickly notice that a large section of the French male population don't know what they're for. Frenchmen demand the freedom to pee wherever they like whether this is away from the traffic or facing into it, whether against lamp-posts or into rivers.

Points system

1 point *for spotting a French male pissing on the side of the road (not much rarity value)*

15 points *for spotting a French male pissing whilst holding a conversation (good one)*

10 points *for spotting a French male pissing whilst smoking a cigarette (doing better)*

20 points *for spotting a French male pissing whilst eating (excellent!)*

So if you can't get the Frenchman to the loo, get the loo to the Frenchman.

> ### Historical Note
> When Paris rioted in 1871 one of the main demands of the protesters was for more public loos so people would stop peeing on the streets. Once the French parliament debated at length whether or not a gentleman in a pissoir should lift his hat to a passing lady he recognised or not.

This was the principle behind the *pissoir* – open-air street urinals, once a common feature in French towns but now gradually being replaced by the fancy *Sanisette* – self cleaning automatic loos.

But there are still times when all the French can offer you is a hole in the ground or a squat loo, but they have a clever knack of disowning them by calling them *toilettes à la turque* – so if you don't like them, blame the Turks.

Where we say bang your head against a brick wall to express frustration at lack of progress, the French say *autant pisser dans un violon* – you may as well piss in a violin – well why not? After all they piss everywhere else.

As Gertrude Stein, a famous American writer who lived in

Paris, said: *'In France one must adapt oneself to the fragrance of a urinal'*

Smells

YOU CAN ALWAYS TELL when a subject is of interest to the French because they have loads of words for it. This is certainly true of verbs that mean to smell or, more literally, to stink. *Puer, refouler, trouilloter, coincer, sclinguer, cocoter......* the list goes on.

Smelliness probably improved for a while when the bidet was invented in the early eighteenth century and kept next to the chamber pot in bedrooms to supplement the very occasional

> **Historical Note**
> *In the old days everyone was pretty pongy but Henri IV, King of France's pong was so bad that Marie de Médici fainted when she was introduced to her future husband.*

bath. But even now Frenchmen have been heard describing fellow Frenchmen as smelling *'like kangaroos kept in cages'* – takes one to know one!

Your average French person only uses 2 and a quarter bars of soap a year, buys a toothbrush once every three years and half of them never brush their teeth before going to bed. Tut, tut! What would the dentist say?

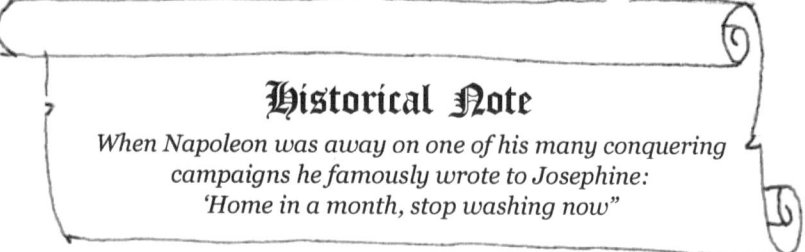

Historical Note
When Napoleon was away on one of his many conquering campaigns he famously wrote to Josephine:
'Home in a month, stop washing now"

The French enjoy body smells and think they're much sexier than the smell of lotions and potions. To stink – p*uer* – is fine, but even better is to smell of goat *(puer le bouc)* or of wild animal *(puer le fauve)* – that's a real turn on.

Bums

CUL , LE DERRIÈRE – whatever you call it, don't underestimate it, the French find many uses for it. Doctors for a start, as many medicines and most jabs get given up the backside. Ouch!

Avoir du cul in French, means you're a lucky bum. *Un tire-au-cul* is a bummer or someone who skives, *un leche cul* is a bum-licker and if you have *du poil au cul* – hair on your bum, then you have guts, according to the French that is.

The French like to tell it as it is – *pécu* (which is short for *le papier-cul)* is literally bum paper which makes sense, after all loo roll isn't for wiping the loo. Whereas in French an old banger of a car is *un vrai tape-cul* – a bum-thumper, which is truer than bone-shaker as we might say. And in French a haw – the prickly fruit of a wild rose – is called *gratte-cul,* bum-scratcher, so presumably the French must put them in their pants.

Farts

FARTING – *FAIRE LE PÉT* – is a French art. If you *péter plus haut que son cul* – that is to fart higher than your bum, then you think too highly of yourself. If you *péter le feu* – that is to fart fire, then you're full of energy. And fritters are called *les pets-de-nonne* – nun's farts!

Les musiciens (musicians) is French slang for beans because of their ability to make you fart.

péter le feu

𝔥istorical 𝔑ote

Merde is sometimes known as le mot de Cambronne – rumour has it that the General who had to surrender to Wellington at Waterloo, famously yelled it out to the British forces.

And finally, shit or merde.

MERDE IS *LES CINQ lettres de France* – France's 5 (as opposed to 4) – letter word. Although it's not as rude as the word shit is in English.

The French love *merde* and find constant use for it:

Merde alors! – shit!, damn!, hell!

Petit merdeux! – you little shit

Quels merdeux! – what brats (shits)

Je suis dans la merde – I'm up shit creek

Or even *merde!* to wish someone luck like we might say 'break a leg'

And it doesn't stop there as *merde* has fathered a family of words:

C'est merdique – awful (like crap)

S'emmerder – to be bored stiff

Je l'emmerde – to hell with him/her

Se demerder – to get out of the shit
La démerde – the art of always getting what you want
Un emmerdement – trouble / a problem
Emmerder – to be annoying, irritating
Un emmerdeur – a pain in the neck
Les merdiers – a mess (the shitpile)

There's even a *merde* word for being annoyed (*emmerdé*) with your mother-in-law (*belle-mère*) – *embellemerdé!*

Historical Note

Napoleon found merde helpul as a put down when he famously said to Talleyrand: 'vous êtes de la merde dans un bas de soie' – you're shit in silk stockings. – Nice one, Boney!

BUT NOT CONTENT WITH one word, the French also have *chier* meaning to crap but this is ruder – *chiottes* is a crude word for the loo (more like the bog) and *un chiant* is a pain in the arse rather than a pain in the neck and should be saved for moments of true annoyance when *merde* simply won't do.

In France you can officially describe something as shit-coloured:

- *caca d'oie* is goose shit colour
- *une coleur pisseuse* is the colour of watery piss.

So there's no need to mince your words when commenting on the colour of a friend's recently painted front room.

A rude reminder

The top five verbs:

Chier – to crap
Pisser – to piss
Gerber – to puke
Roter – to burp
Péter – to fart

Miam miam!
(Yum, yum!)
Foody French

CHAPTER TEN
Miam miam! (Yum, yum!)

> 'Dis-moi ce que tu manges, je te dirai
> ce que tu es.'
> – Tell me what you eat and I'll tell you what you are.
> *(famous French foodie)*

SO WHAT DO THEIR favourite dishes tell you about the French? Well, they eat 40,000 tons of snails (*l'escargot*) each year. Of course first they have to salt the snails so they excrete their slime and then they cook them alive.

And there are those highly prized truffles -, stinky lumps of fungus dug up by sex-crazed pigs.

We mustn't forget *pâté de foie gras* – do you know where that comes from? Do you really, really want to know? OK, a duck or a goose is force fed maize (through a funnel to stop it gagging) at least four times a day until its liver is so horribly overgrown that it nearly explodes. Nice, eh?

And of course they love garlic, they even chew it raw to keep the flies off.. ...although you'd think they might want to catch the flies for some yummy French dish or other.

Beurk!

OF COURSE FOOD IS no joking matter, to the French that is. It's been said that the French live to eat, the Germans eat to live and the English eat to die. The French believe their cuisine is way ahead of the rest, which in fairness it probably is. The only other cuisine to come close is the Chinese and they have much in common. Like the Chinese, the French eat anything that swims, flies, slides, hops or, as they say in China, gets the sun on its back. In 1870 when Paris was under siege, the Parisians ate everything that moved , they even killed the elephant from the Paris zoo and ate it. And they don't like to waste bodyparts – tongues, cheeks, tails, organs, ears, brains – they'll hoof the lot!

Take the poor pig, not much wastage here. They'll eat the *pieds de porc* – trotters, the *oreilles de porc* – ears, the *queue de porc* – tail. And don't be fooled by *fromage de tête* (head cheese) and order it for your cheese course, it's potted pig's head.

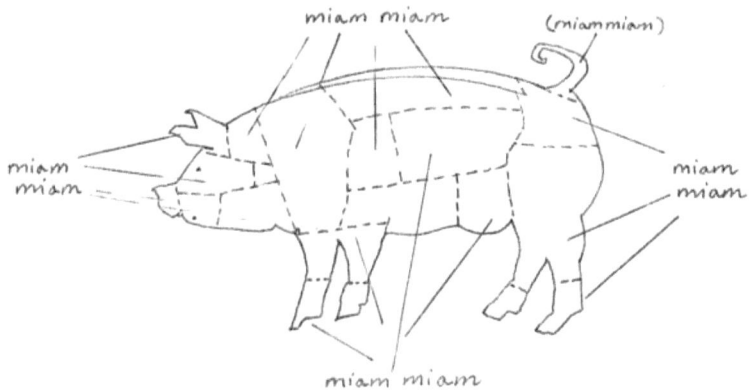

It's amazing what treats French 5-star restaurants have in store. Dishes to watch out for on French menus include *mou* (lung), *gras double* (tripe), *cervelle* (brain), *ris* (pancreas), *fraise* (general innards) and last but not least *rognons blancsprimelles* (testicles). Watch out if you're vegetarian. For the rest of you, don't forget lots of hand to mouth kissing actions – '*miam, miam!*' (delicious!) when you do encounter any of these. (If you really, really need it then *beurk!* is yuk!)

Now we all know the French like a frog or two *(les grenouilles)* but did you know they consume over 200 million a year? And they're not French (the frogs that is). Most are imported from South-East Asia and the USA.

American frogs got their own back when the Hollywood film cannibal, Hannibal Lecter, famously said:

'I just love the French. They taste like chicken!'

The French take their meat extremely seriously and butchers specialise in one or other variety. They'll sell either red meat or pork or poultry but rarely together. And then there are of course *Les boucheries chevalines* – yup, you guessed it, horse butchers – easy to spot as they usually have a large horse's head above the door. Not as popular as they were, but still common in the countryside. Horsemeat is cheap and healthy and was heartily recommended by Napoleon's doctor to see you through a Russian winter.

IN FRANCE THEY SAY "a good meal must always end with a good cheese" so here are a few to chose from:
- *Crottin* – literally 'dung' and what the French call very smelly goat's cheese that comes in a dark dollop and stinks
- *Le Puant de Lille* – a cheese that smells of ammonia and is called the Stinker of Lille
- And *Comté* cheese which is best eaten at least two and a half years after it's been made

> ### Historical Note
> France's great soldier, war time leader and post war President General de Gaulle (1890-1970), might have been on to something when he famously said: 'How can you govern a country which has 246 varieties of cheese?' To which Churchill replied 'But how can you let a nation that produces so many cheeses fall to the Nazis?'

FRENCH TOWNS and many villages have a market (*marché*) often on a Wednesday or Saturday, selling and celebrating local produce. Turn up early enough and you can sample, slurp, sniff and prod the lot, there's none of this hands off approach. Towns take real pride in their regional specialities – there's a Museum of Mustard and there's even a Festival of Snails which just goes to show that they'll happily celebrate

Fly pie

the humblest of creatures that will punish itself in the name of great French cuisine.

The French put taste way before safety so it's not surprising that they are obsessed with their digestion and are always complaining of *une crise de foie* – a liver crisis. They should just be thankful that they weren't born as a French goose being prepared for foie gras – or maybe it's brought on by fear that in their next life they just might be.

Forget fish 'n chips and enjoy your meal. *Bon ap!*

Bouffe! (Grub!)
Table Manners

CHAPTER ELEVEN
Bouffe! *(Grub!)*

S LANG FOR FOOD OR a meal is *la bouffe* (grub) and the French eat out at *un resto* or *un bistro*. We may think café and restaurant are typical French words but they don't use them much.

Here's an old French joke:

What's the difference between a Frenchman and an Englishman getting ready for a good meal? The Frenchman takes off his jacket and the Englishman crosses the Channel.

The French, including chefs and waiters, take their lunches so seriously that some restaurants close for lunch.

And watch out for the waiters. Being a waiter in France is a profession. The real ones are easy to tell apart from the

students earning some holiday cash, they wear a white shirt, black trousers and waistcoat with pockets full of small change.

They're nearly always male and they're arrogant, rude, grumpy and completely hyper, unlike the students who are usually friendly but a bit hopeless. And like other French professions, they like to go on strike. Here are three reasons why they're so grumpy:

1. The all important tip was usually a 10 francs coin and is now 1 euro (which is worth less than 10 francs) so they feel the whole

of Europe is out to cheat them.

2. They get addressed as 'garçon' which means boy!

3. And of course they hate foreigners (even though a lot of them are foreign).

I T'S WELL KNOWN THAT IF you don't use their language they'll rip you off. So, if you want a normal drink and a normal sized bill remember to:

- order coffee not tea (tea is seen as poncey and English and is twice the price of coffee)
- order *un crème* for a white coffee (or *un grand crème* for a big one) and only *café au lait* for a litre of milky slop
- say *un express* not expresso (that's Italian and French waiters **only** speak French)
- be particular – if you want it strong ask for it to be *serré*
- and if it's weak or watery make sure you say *du pipi d'âne* or *du pipi de chat* – donkey's or cat's piss loudly and with a look of complete exasperation

pipi de chat

- if you say *une bière* for a beer you'll end up with a large and expensive bottle of imported beer, say *un demi* or *à présion* and you'll get a normal half pint glass of draught
- and if you want a jug of water ask for *une carafe d'eau* (jug of water) or the slang *la flotte* not *de l'eau* (water) which is a prompt for mineral water

IT'S A GOOD IDEA TO TRY to keep French waiters on side. So, call them *Monsieur!* or raise your arm and say *s'il vous plaît* but never *Garçon!* Don't ask for your steak to be well done (*bien cuit* or as the French call it, BBC *bien, bien cuit* for the Brits). Don't say *connard* (see chapter 5) when you're trying to order *canard* (duck). And never ask them for ketchup or they'll think you're completely below contempt. In fact they even have a phrase in French: *'à bon appetit il ne faut point de sauce'* – a good appetite needs no sauce.

They may say *le client est roi* (the customer is king) in France, but never forget what they did to their King. So if you feel your temperature rising (or the mustard going up your nose which is the French expression for losing your cool), you can always head off for a Big Mac. Contrary to what the French like us to think they love *le fast food*. McDonalds is known rather affectionately as *McDo* (pronounced Mac Dough).

They also like us to think that they never miss a meal, they live to eat rather than eat to live, they savour every morsel, they never snack and that they never, ever eat in front of the telly.

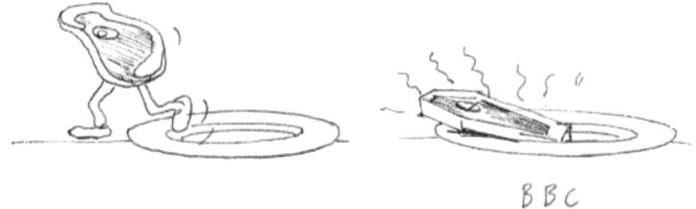

But is this really true?

For a start breakfast is usually skipped or eaten on the hoof. Croissants, *pain au chocolat* and brioche are special treats, as there's no time to queue up at the bakery on a weekday. Usually it's just yesterday's stale crust or long life bread and fiercely strong coffee to make them even more foul tempered in the morning rush. They don't go in for fresh milk (you'll only find it in supermarkets where enough tourists shop), they have UHT long life and flavoured milk drinks instead (which kids drink out of a bowl and dunk their bread into).

DESPITE ALL THE RESTOS and bistros, 70% of the French eat lunch at home during the week. And since they have a word for snacking – *gôuter* – they must do it. A popular (after school) snack is a baguette with a bar of chocolate in between. In fact *casse-croûte* has come to mean snack, the *croûte* is the end of the baguette and breaking it off (*casse*) to have with cheese or chocolate, coined the phrase. Where we might have something like beans on toast, they'll have *jambon purée* – ham and mash. So maybe they're not so different after all.

Le Pain

IF EVER THERE WAS a French institution it's *La Boulangerie*. *Boulangeries* are so sacred that they're the only places where the French will queue, well queue French-style that is, usually several people thick shuffling along with their noses and toes. France simply wouldn't be France without them. At least that's what Napoleon thought when he invented them. After the revolution he decreed that every French village had to have a bakery baking two or three times a day and selling fresh bread daily. There are still over 35,000 of them.

> **Historical Note**
> It is said that sliced bread was invented during the French Revolution to feed Louis XVI in prison (obviously before his head was chopped off) to stop his supporters smuggling messages in a loaf to help him escape.

IN FACT NAPOLEON declared that all citizens should eat the same bread and so regulated its size and weight. Even today a baguette is 80cm long, weighs 250g and its price is set by the State – so check yours out! They say the baguette is that length and shape so Napoleon's soldiers could carry them in their trousers. Give it a try and see how you get on.

French breads are named by their shape: *baguette* (stick), *croissant* (crescent) *ficelle* (string), *flûte* (flute), *boule* (ball) and *épi* (spike) – try that one down your trousers for special effect.

What you'll never find, at least not over many dead French bodies, is a *boulangerie* selling sliced white bread.

Tchin Tchin!
(Cheers!)
Grape Talk

CHAPTER TWELVE
Tchin Tchin! (Cheers!)

THE FRENCH LOVE TO drink wine and have been known to drink it at any time of day – even with breakfast. The average French person drinks 64 litres of wine a year, that's 1¼ litres a week. So to act like a Frenchman you would need to say *Tchin tchin!* and down a bottle (or two). This will also help with mastering the art of gesticulation (Chapter 3: *Bof!)* and insults (Chapter 5 : *Quel ***!).*

French children develop a taste for it fairly early on. In the country there has always been a tradition of giving children *du vin coupé* (wine diluted with water) and although the legal age for drinking is 16, it's not really enforced and many places serve alcohol to under 16s.

Wine falls into two categories – plonk for getting plastered and fine wine for getting pretentious.

Plonk

*P*INARD IS French slang for wine. Real plonk is *la piquette*. Check out what others are drinking – the money back bottles with raised stars round the neck is the plonkiest plonk.

Then there's *vin de table* (table wine) and *vin de pays* (country wine). In general the more detail there is about where precisely the wine comes from and the vineyard where the grapes are grown, the better and posher the wine will be.

If the bottlers haven't got a clue where it comes from and it's mixed up with grapes from other regions it's bottled up and sold cheap. The French call red table wine, *le gros rouge* (thick

le gros rouge

red wine) or to give it its full name, *le gros rouge qui tache et qui pousse au crime (*the thick red wine that stains and incites to crime).

You can fill up large plastic jerricans from local producers and cars have even been known to run off the stuff.

If you drink too much you are *paf* or *bourré* (plastered) and there's even a beaujolais wine called *Pisse-Dur* (Pissing Hard). A gdb is French for a hangover – *gueule de bois* (mouth of wood).

Posh wine

POSH WINES GET VERY complicated which is why there are so many wine experts around. Remember, experts like to keep things complicated or they'd be out of a job. You might think it's simple – red wine is made from red grapes and white wine from white grapes but did you know that you can also make white wine from red grapes?

The French have a phrase '*à bon vin point d'enseigne*' – a

good wine needs no sign but *appellation contrôlée* on the label is a sign that you are drinking something posher. This is the French state's way of making sure that the wine comes from the wine producing region it says it comes from.

Don't be fooled by *Chateau-Lapompe*, it's slang for tap water – Pump Castle! *Champomy* is a bubbly non-alcoholic apple-based champagne for kids and you can always *faire péter le bouchon* that is make the cork fart (pop as we would say).

FINE WINE APPRECIATION, so they tell us, is all in the nose. And wine tasting (*dégustation*) has a language all of its own. First of all, you never, ever talk of a wine's smell. Of course you *are* talking about its smell but you must always refer to it as the 'aroma' or 'bouquet'. Wines are spoken of as being forward on the nose (strong) or behind on the nose (not so strong).

And that's before you start on what it smells of (sorry, I mean describe its 'aroma'). A wood on a crisp winter's day? A rabbit on heat? Unleaded petrol? An old leather belt? Freshly laundered underwear? Rotten fish? Smelly socks?

Monsieur le Dégustier

Historical Note

Not everything that's posh has always been that way – a Dom Pérignon champagne might be a status symbol now but over 300 years ago it was a simple invention by a monk who wanted to put some sparkle into cheap white wine for local weddings.

HERE ARE THE KEY steps if you fancy becoming a dégustier (a wine taster) although it doesn't include how to grow that nose:

1. Check the cork

2. Pour (with a certain flourish)

3. Peer suspiciously at the look of it in the glass

4. Swirl

5. Slurp

6. Swill it around in the mouth (try not to dribble at this stage)

7. Spit (projecting it in a perfect arch into something that can act as a spitoon – an open handbag for example)

8. Say what ever comes into your head about the aroma, bouquet, nose etc. The more outlandish the better.

Tchao! (Hi!)
Saying Hello

CHAPTER THIRTEEN
Tchao! (Hi!)

O NE THING WORTH KNOWING about the French is they like to touch each other (a lot). This may well extend to you so be prepared. If it's a first encounter you may be lucky and get away with a handshake, but what they really like is an excuse for kisses, a hug or both. Keeping your hands in your pockets is the height of rudeness, you need to get them out and fling them about.

Warn a younger brother or sister that if they get patted on the head and called *puce* which means flea, they should not bare their teeth or try to bite, but smile sweetly, as this is in fact a French endearment.

But it's kissing where many a visitor first comes unstuck. What you need to realise is that everyone does it – French Presidents, French soldiers, French teachers, French teenagers. In fact French

teenagers have turned kissing into an art form all of their own. Making their exit can take half the night as they say *salut* and then kiss everyone in sight.

You don't need to fancy someone to kiss them, you don't even need to like them. It's just the touchy-feely French way of saying hi and bye.

But you need to get it right otherwise you'll be sending out all kinds of signals you never intended and efforts to embrace will only act to embarrass. So here are the rules:

1. Don't overdo it – a light brush of the cheek will do.

2. **Never, ever just the one kiss** – at least two and, this is the complicated bit, it can be three or four depending on the region.

3. **Left cheek, right cheek, left cheek.**

However this last rule leaves the tricky problem of your left or their left so just look confident and take whatever's offered. Fingers crossed there'll be no nose collisions. And whatever you do, try not to blush.

STILL IT COULD BE WORSE, at least they've dropped the rule about newly married couples in France having to stand naked outdoors while the groom kissed the bride's left foot and big toe (OK, that was about 400 years ago)

So not only do you have to get hands out of pockets and make physical contact but you're also expected to make eye contact and greet everyone, everywhere. Instead of saying something is

as 'easy as pie', the French saying is 'it's as easy as saying hello'. There are greetings for first-thing, mid-thing, early-thing, late-thing. The French will wish you a good journey, a good meal, a good weekend, a good week and probably even a good trip to the loo.

Luckily *ça va* is on hand which can be muttered or mumbled both as greeting and response. It's rather like saying OK? OK. In Paris cool dudes have taken to re-arranging the letters so instead of ça va they now say ça av. *Salut* is also pretty universal – on the plus side you can use it pretty much at anytime, even to say goodbye, but be warned, it usually comes with lots of kisses.

I F YOU WANT TO BE more English about it, *Hello* has become perfectly acceptable although you'll have to try the French pronunciation which is more like saying it back to front – *ell oh. Bye bye!* Is fast catching on too. And if you want to be more Italian then there's *Ciao!* – beloved of all Italians – the French have nicked it and re-christened it *Tchao!*

Street Talk

Hé! is like our Yo! – a good way to get attention quickly

Quoi de neuf (what's up?)

Ça boume (how's it going?)

Ça cartonne? (doing well?)

You've mastered the kissing, you've got a few greetings up your sleeve but the French have one final pitfall to catch you out. It's the tricky business of you: is it *tu* or is it *vous?*

THEY TEACH YOU AT SCHOOL that the basic rule is to call all animals and everyone your age *tu*.

But if in doubt because they look old, or...

▶ scary

▶ you're meeting them for the first time

▶ they're your teacher

▶ your boss

▶ you need to be especially polite and respectful to get a nice present / talk your way out of trouble / get a good grade etc

go for *vous*

So...what would you call a very old elephant? Tu ☐ Vous ☐

And...what would you call a scary teenage goth? Tu ☐ Vous ☐

THE FRENCH LIKE A BIT OF formality. Children address adults as *Monsieur* or *Madame,* which is like saying Sir in English. Even at work the French often address each other as *Monsieur X* or *Madame Y.* To be *tutoi-ed* – that is being called *tu* – is a sign of being totally accepted and a part of the family. But there are still couples in France who've never called each other *tu* in all their married lives.

And written greetings?

No problem... if you sign off a letter in France, there's none of this sloppy 'best wishes', 'kind regards', you're expected to go the whole hog and write:

Nous vous prions d'agréer, Monsieur (or Madame) l'assurance de nos sentiments respectueux – We beg you to believe in the assurance of our respectful sentiments. How's that for a mouthful?

And you don't send cards at Christmas or for birthdays but you do send them at New Year, got it?

But the French do love presents, so bring them something gift-wrapped and you'll find that all *faux pas* (false steps) are quickly forgiven.

Puce! (Flea!)
Kids Speak

CHAPTER FOURTEEN
Puce! (Flea!)

THE FRENCH MAY CLAIM to like children and even give the Mums of large families a medal on Mother's day, (bronze for 4 or 5 children, silver for 6 or 7 and a gold medal for 8 or more!), but they have so many different ways of saying 'you brat' or 'brats' that it's difficult to believe. *Les gosses, les gamins, les momes, les chipies, les lardons, les mioches, les marmots, les mouflets, les rejetons, les moutards* are all fairly insulting by themselves and are often preceded by *sales* which means dirty or ghastly... And then there's *la petite frappe* which means hoodlum, *les morveux* which means the snotty-nosed and *les chiards*, the crappers.

And if they are feeling indulgent they'll pat a child on the head and call it *puce* which means flea. So if you get called a flea consider yourself lucky, it could be so much worse.

But if someone wants to shake your fleas – *secouer les puces à quelqu'un,* it means they want to tell you off.

They even have a phrase for adults who are still wild and unruly – *enfant terrible* (terrible child) for which there is no age limit.

Children can always act up to meet French expectations of little snotty-nosed crappers. Here's some lingo to get up their noses:

Aie! (ow)
Ouille! (ouch!)
Beurk! (yuk!)

J'ai bobo (babyspeak for I'm hurt)
J'ai toto (babyspeak for I have lice)
Pipi (babyspeak for pee)
Caca (babyspeak for poo)
Le loulou (babyspeak for snot)
Hi, hi (boo hoo)

Applying French sound effects to everyday life is another sure-fire way to annoy. Tintin and Asterix comics can provide a good supply.

- For crash / bang sounds use *badaboum!* and *patatras!*
- For splash! use *flac!* or *plouf!*
- Phew! is *ouf!*
- If you sneeze then the sound to make is *achoum!*
- Knock, knock jokes in French need to start with *toc-toc-toc*
- *Boum!* is bang whereas bang-bang! is *pan pan!*
- And the sound of a French siren is *pimpom, pimpom*

MEANWHILE IF OTHERS are rabbiting on you can try either *taratata!* (which means rubbish!) or *patati patata* (which means blah, blah, blah...)

If you find yourself playing games with the French kids, here are a few words that might come in handy:

Cache-cache – hide and seek
Pouce! (meaning thumb!) is Pax! or time out
Dépêche-toi!! is hurry up! Or *grouille-toi!* which is get a move on!
Attends-moi! is wait for me!
Qui gagne? is who's winning?
C'est à toi! is your turn!
Attrape! is catch!
Lance-toi! – just do it!

A typical French party game is to hang a bag of *bonbons* (sweets) from a tree and you have to try to break it open by throwing things at it and shaking the tree.

F RENCH KIDS HAVE a riddle about family relations which goes like this:

Mon père est maire (sounds like mère – my father is my mother but means my father is mayor*), j'ai un cousin qui est frère* (I have a cousin who is a brother – as in monk), *mon frère est masseur* (sounds like my brother is my sister – *ma soeur* – but means my brother gives massages) *ma tante est soeur* (my aunt is sister – as in a nun) *et mon oncle est une tante* (and my uncle is an aunt – slang for gay).

But if you've had enough of drunks going *patati patata* or playing with French kids then declare *au dodo!* (off to bed!)

Ouah! Ouah!
(Woof! Woof!)
Animal Talk

CHAPTER FIFTEEN
Ouah! Ouah! (Woof! Woof!)

THE FRENCH MAY NOT love children as much as they say but they certainly love animals (when they're not shooting them that is). Over half of all French homes have a pet, which is more than any other European country, and many households have both dogs and cats.

There are 10 million dogs in France. And this isn't just a country thing – Paris is a city of dog owners. It has been estimated that Paris has over 200,000 dogs which dump 15 tonnes of dog poo on the streets each year. So be careful not to end up a casualty statistic with the other 650 or so Parisians who end up in hospital each year having skidded on dog poo.

The French can be snobbish about dog breeds and favour ones that have been around for centuries. Poodles are the nation's favourite mutt, one in six French dogs is a poodle.

> ### Historical Note
> *The French love affair with the poodle has being going on since the eighteenth century when they were the lapdogs of the Louis'.*

Since the French have a pronunciation problem with 'w', a dog's bark is *ouah! ouah!* rather than woof! woof! Other animal sounds include *miaou* for cats, *bêêê* for sheep and *meuh* for cows – sounds familiar, but less familiar is coin-coin for ducks and *cocorico* for cocks.

A French animal joke:

The brothers and sisters were quarrelling:

– *Quel âne!* (ass!)

– *Tête de cochon!* (pig-head!)

– *Espèce de dinde!* (turkey!)

Their mother arrives and cries – *Oh, la ferme!*

(Oh shut up you animals!)

La ferme means farm and is slang for shut up.

THE COCK HAS a special significance in France, it's their national symbol. It was the Romans who called the French *Gauls* which comes from *gallus* which is Latin for cock. The Romans might have been on to something as cocks are noisy, vain and like a good fight.

Insects can, in France, bring good or bad luck. A ladybird landing on your finger is good luck and so is seeing a spider in the evening – although seeing a spider in the morning is definitely bad luck.

And April Fool's Day is a fishy event known as *Poisson d'Avril* (April Fish). The papers carry fish-based spoofs and children try to pin paper fish on each others' backs.

THE FRENCH LANGUAGE has some great animal phrases. Dogs may be the nation's favourite pet but that doesn't mean they have favoured status. To describe something as *de chien* (of dog) means really low and lousy like *vie de chien* – a dog's life. *Un temps de chien* (time of dog) means bad weather, *malade comme un chien* means as sick as a dog and *avoir un mal de chien* means to face great difficulties. But for some reason known only to the French, *avoir du chien* (to have dog) means to be chic and sexy.

We might not be able to teach an old dog new tricks but in France they can't teach a monkey how to make faces – *on n'apprend pas à un singe comment faire la grimace*.

Where we would describe plain speaking as calling a spade a spade, the French say *appeler un chat un chat* – to call a cat a

une vache à roulettes

cat and a frog in your throat is, in French, a cat down the throat – *avoir un chat dans la gorge*. Meanwhile *donner sa langue au chat* (to give one's tongue to the cat) means to give up. So try giving up calling a cat a cat because you've got a frog in your throat.

And raining cats and dogs is *pleuvoir comme vache qui pisse* – to rain like a cow pissing. *Vaches* (cows) is also slang for cops (like we might say pigs) and *une vache à roulettes* (a cow on wheels) is a motorbike cop. French police are also known as *poulets* (chickens) but don't call them a cow or a chicken to their face because, unlike our police, they carry guns and live ammunition.

pleuvoir comme vache qui pisse

To say 'when pigs will fly' (that is, never) in French you'd say *quand les poules auront des dents* – when hens have teeth.

Here are a few more animal sayings:

- *Faire mouche (To do fly)* To get the bullseye
- *Poser un lapin (To put down a rabbit)* To stand someone up
- *Une poule mouillée (A wet chicken)* A coward
- *Un drôle de zèbre (A funny zebra)* A peculiar person

- *Ne pas être piqué des vers* (*Not to be picked by the worms*) To be first rate
- *C'est super chouette!* (*It is super owl!*) It is fantastic!
- *Avoir le cafard* (*To have the cockroach*) To have the blues
- *Faire un canard* (*To make a duck*) To hit a wrong note
- *Pas folle la guêpe* (*Not crazy the wasp*) Not born yesterday
- *Tuer les mouches à quinze pas* (*To kill flies at 15 paces*) To have bad breath

And a bat in French is rather appropriately called *une chauve-souris* – a bald mouse.

Branché! (Cool!)
Plugged-in French

CHAPTER SIXTEEN
Branché! (Cool!)

So what's cool or plugged in – *branché* – as the French would say? First *la zic* (music). France has long been famous for its bum-hugging trouser-wearing, sexy, male smoochers and crooners – Sacha Distel, Charles Aznavour, Serge Gainsbourg – and with song titles such as I Love You,

When I Fall in Love, SHE, You and Me, Love and Goodbye Darling, you can guess the rest. Not very *branché*.

There's always been a tradition of *chansons* (songs) and *chanteur/chanteuse* (singers) in France. So when Jean-Philippe Smet wanted to launch himself as France's first serious rocker, he changed his name to the American-sounding Johnny Halliday to borrow a bit of trans-Atlantic cool. He knew he'd never make it if he sounded too French.

MORE RECENTLY FRENCH music has become big internationally in two areas: techno and rap. *Air*, an electro-pop music duo has become the most successful French band in the world and other cutting-edge techno bands include *Miossec, Dominique A* and *Daft Punk,* the disco kings of France and MTV. *Daft Punk* were cool and groovy until they really sold out first by making an advert for Gap to flog jeans and then, as if that wasn't bad enough, they designed a coffee table for Habitat – how uncool is that?

France is also home to the greatest number of rap artists after America with *MC Solaar* leading the pack. American hip hop with French lyrics meets North Africa. *Raï* is a new sound that mixes old and modern African beats. But as with many things in France, the French State won't leave the music scene alone. On the longest day of the year – 21stJune – there is a *Fête de la Musique* when amateur musicians throughout the land are encouraged to get out there and jam. There's also a law that 40% of French radio output has to be French music or else sung in French. This is to stop too much foreign influence since many French teenagers now wake up and go to bed with the radio on. It has led to some foreign bands recording in French just to get more airtime. Stations to check out and see if you can spot any include:

Sky Rock (rap)
RNB
NRJ (dance)
Le Mouv (funky and aimed at 18-24 yr olds)
Oui FM (Paris only)

The good news is that there's no problem discussing la zic if you want to be ultra-branché with the French:

Dance is *la dance*
Hip hop is *le hip hop*
House is *la house* (not la maison)
Jazz is *le jazz*
Pop is *la pop*
Rap is *le rap*
Reggae is *le reggae*
Rock is *le rock*
Techno is *la techno*

SO, WHEN THEY'RE NOT listening to music what do *les ados* (teenagers, short for adolescents) get up to? Well first there is a lot of school. Eight hours a week more than in the UK to be precise. They also count their classes backwards which can be confusing for us – the first year of primary is Year 11, the last is Year 7. In Year 6 they start secondary school which goes on until Year 3 when you can leave (aged 15) or go on to *Lycée* for Yr 2 and Year 1 to do *le bac (baccalauréat)*. There are exams at the end of each year and if you fail a year then you have to stay down and repeat it. So if you meet a 13 year old in Year 4, don't treat him or her as a hopeless failure, just remember that's how they count the years in France.

But the French being French means even school kids get two hours for lunch. Does it really take two hours to eat the French equivalent of chicken nuggets and beans? Or maybe it's just an excuse to get away from school for a bit as French school kids can go home or even to the local café. On Wednesday afternoons there's no school so if you see a lot of school age children hanging around street corners, it's not them skiving, it's the teachers. And on top of all that they have the longest school holidays in the world, 117 days or nearly a third of the year off! They'll tell you it's to compensate for having to work so much harder at school.

When in France you could try claiming a few extra rights. This is what French kids are allowed to do:

At 14 yrs
- The right to a summer job
- The right to ride a moped (under 50cc)
- The right to go into a bar without an adult

At 15 yrs
- The right to have sex with people 15 and over
- The right to see a Doctor on your own
- The right for girls to marry with parental consent (boys not until 18)

At 16 yrs
- The right to leave school and work
- The right to ride a motorbike (under 125cc)
- The right to learn to drive a car
- The right to drink alcohol in a bar

At 17 yrs
- The right to ride a motorbike with a license

LIKE ALL TEENAGERS, French teenagers like to chill out watching TV – lots of TV – American soaps, chat shows, gameshows, talent shows and reality shows. Programmes like Fame Academy, Big Brother (which they call Loft Story) and Celebrity Big Brother (which they call Nice People). They even have a name for these shows – *la télé-poubelle* – trash TV. Non-French shows are all dubbed and it can be fun listening to a famous actor speaking French with a strange voice. Dubbed children can sound particularly strange since they usually use adults pretending to sound like children. The popular channels with ads are M6 and TF1. Public channels like the BBC are France 2 (general interest), France 3 (national and regional), Arté (cultural) and France 5 (educational). Canal + is the main cable channel and Canal J is the cable channel for kids.

And when they're not watching *la télé-poubelle* they're reading magazines and comic books – *la bande dessinée*. Unlike our comics, some of these *bande dessinée* are pretty *branché* and worth checking out.

And then there are those moments when they are literally *branché*, that is plugged in. The computer is *l'ordi*, short for *l'ordinateur*, but with things technical, like music, English will get you quite far. The campaign to get the French to use the term courriel instead of email was a dismal failure and President Mitterand was heard to say wistfully, *'must we give orders to our computers in English?'*

Video is vidéo

TV is télé

Playstation is playstation

Xbox is *Xbox*–Gameboy is *gameboy*
iPod is *iPod*
Modem is *Modem*
E-mail is *E-mail* or *mèl* for short
CDs are *CDs*
DVDs are *DVDs*
Walkman is *walkman*
MP3 is *MP3*
To surf is *surfer*
Website is *site*
Cable or broadband is *câble*
And to connect on-line is *connecter*

In addition all you need to know is *souris* which is French for mouse and *mon ordi a planté* for when the computer crashes.

Popular games are *Les Sims, FIFA Soccer* (where you're the coach) and *Gran Turismo*.

Here's some more lingo to help you play:

Vise! – aim
Tire! – hit him
Marque! – score
Saute! – jump
Fonce! – quick
Tue-le! – kill him
Rallume! – restart

But when it's all over it's back to English with *Game over*.

Google, Altavista and Yahoo all have French versions, popular portals that provide email are iFrance, Wanadoo and Club Internet and mobile phone networks you'll see are SFR, GSM and Orange.

Like *ordi* (short for *ordinateur*), it's *branché* to slice words in half. And it's not just teenagers who do this, words are getting the chop all the time.

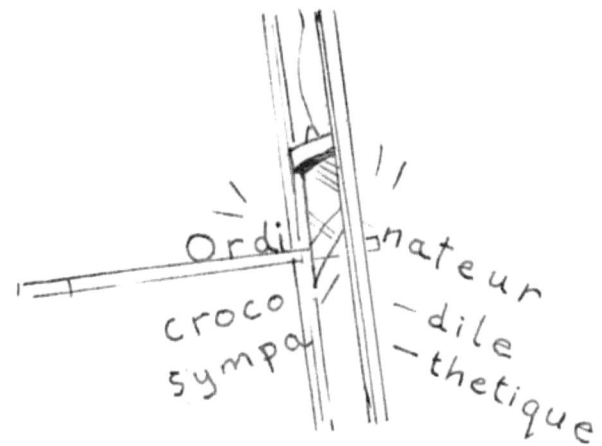

- Instead of *sympathtique* for friendly and nice say *sympa*
- Instead of *rigolote* for funny say *rigolo*
- Instead of *crocodile* say *croco*
- Instead of *intellectuel* for clever say *intello*
- Instead of *dictionnaire* for dictionnary say *dico*
- Instead of *frigidaire* for fridge say *frigo*
- Instead of *géographie* say *géo*

Get the idea?

And to abbreviate French even more there's French text messaging:

- **slt** salut (hi)
- **G** j'ai (I'm)
- **C** c'est (it is)
- **PK** pourquoi (why)
- **Bi1** bien (good)
- **cv** ça va (how are you?)
- **jvb** je vais bien (I'm fine)
- **apLER moi** appelez-moi (call me)
- **Bjr** bonjour (hello)
- **dsl** – desolé (really sorry)
- **BL é 5pa** belle et sympa (beautiful and nice)
- **RAS** rien à signaler (nothing)
- **tu vi1** tu viens? (Are you coming?)
- **je C pas** Je sais pas (Don't know)
- **Je t'M** je t'aime (I love you)
- **Cpa5p** c'est pas sympa (that's not nice)

–**keske C**	Qu'est-ce que c'est? (what is it?)
–**LC moi 1 msg**	Laissez-moi un message (leave me a message)
–**dak**	D'accord (OK)
–**I'S tomB**	Laisse tomber (no problem)
–**@+**	À plus tard (see you later)
–**@2m1**	À demain (see you tomorrow)
–**A12C4**	À un de ces quatres (see you)
–**MDR**	mort de rire (laugh out loud)
–**kekina**	Qu'est-ce qu'il qu'il y a? (Are you OK?)
–**koi29**	Quoi de neuf? (what's up?)

Streetwise lingo

And don't forget, if you want to sound cool use the street slang - *argot* . This started off as the secret code of beggars and thieves so that they would not be understood by others. In English slang is often sexual and offensive, in France it's just alternatives for everyday words which everyone uses for everything.

French has masses of slang, simple nouns like bed or shoe can have over a dozen slang versions.

And then there is *verlan* which is used a lot in rap and is literally backslang – the word *verlan* swops around the syllables of *l'envers* which actually means back to front. A good example is *meuf* which is *verlan* slang for *femme* – woman and then some people have turned that back to front again into *feumeu*.

So for some streetwise slang: a guy is *un mec,* mates are *les copains, du fric* is dosh, *les flics* are the cops, *une seche* is a ciggy and parents are *les vieux* (the old).

Ouais! (YessSSS!)
Sporting French

CHAPTER SEVENTEEN
Ouais! (YesssSS!)

Football

FLING THOSE OUTSTRETCHED arms up into the air and shout *OUAIS!!* Yes – success!! This is what the whole of France did in 1998 when not only did they host the football World Cup, but they won it. Zinedine Zidane (the captain), Fabien Barthez (the goalie) and the French national team – *les Bleus* (who wear blue) – became worldwide household names. *Zizou Président* (Zidane's nickname) was beamed onto the Arc de Triomphe and the whole of France basked in the reflected glory.

Other great French footballing heroes, many of whom are more associated with British football than French, include Arsene Wenger (manager of Arsenal), Thierry Henri, Patrick Vieira (both play for Arsenal), Eric Cantona (played for Man U) and

Jacques Santini (Spurs coach). *Ligue 1*(League) is their Premier division and the *Coupe de France* is the French cup. Their Man U and Arsenal are Olympique de Marseille (OM) & Paris Saint Germain (PSG), the two biggest clubs in France.

Football was imported into France in the late nineteenth century by the French middle classes but didn't really take off as a national sport until between the wars. The French have added their own style to the game with poetry writing players and coaches who are more likely to quote philosophy than yell at their team.

The French state sponsor football: the *Institut National du Football* is a system for coaching young talent and *Clairefontaine* is a national training centre near Paris. But since French clubs can't afford to keep their best players, it's a coaching system that acts as a great nursery developing player's skills for the rest of Europe's great clubs.

French football fans are *les supporters* but the ones who are really fanatical are known as *le Kop*.

LIKE ENGLISH FOOTBALL matches, French games are pretty expressive events, so you need to know the lingo. The combination of *foutre* (rude verb see Chapter 5: *Quel ****) with *merde* (5-letter word see Chapter 9: *Pouah!*) gives us *foutre la merde* which means causing aggro at football matches.

Essential speak for le foot:

1. Excited

Bouffez-les! – get them!

Allez! –go!

Faire une passe! – pass the ball!

But! – goal!

2. When winning

Extra, ce but! – great goal!

Magnifique passe! – great pass

Boulet! – powerful kick!

Bravo, le gardien – great save, goalie

3. When losing
Un arbitre fou! – crazy referee
Degueulasse! – foul!
Péno! – penalty!
Immanquable! – unmissable!
Va te coucher – you're useless (go to bed)
Quel nul! – he sucks!
Quel enculé! / merde! – he's a ****!

Groans and general sounds of pain and anguish – French equivalents of aaaargh!:

▶ aie!   ▶ ouille!   ▶ beuh!   ▶ berk!

Rugby

LIKE FOOTBALL, RUGBY was brought over from England by the Victorians. Rugby took off amongst the poor workers in the wine trade in the south—west of France where it's still really big and the region is known as *L'Ovalie* – land of the oval ball. Because the cock is the national symbol of France, French supporters have been known to smuggle cockerels into matches and then let them loose on the rugby pitch both before and during matches. So instead of chasing streakers off the pitch it was more likely to be a flapping, squawking cockerel.

Le quinze de France – or the French national rugby team,

Dieu de stade

won the Six Nations and completed a Grand Slam in both 2002 and 2004. They have always been notorious for getting sent off the pitch and have made themselves even more notorious by posing nude for calendars each year since 2001. The calendars, called *Dieux du Stade* (Gods of the Stadium) are in big demand and for those particularly turned on there is even a DVD of the making of the calendars.

Pétanque

NOW FOR something a bit less raunchy – *pétanque* (or *boules,* meaning balls). Along with kicking a ball, throwing balls at a target is one of the oldest games in the world.

The Egyptians did it, the Greeks did it and the Romans did it between wars with coconuts brought back from North Africa. It was banned during the Renaissance because it was so popular that it distracted from important military pursuits like archery; it was also condemned by the Catholic Church for encouraging gambling.

The game first took off at the end of the nineteenth century in

> ## Historical Note
> *Sir Francis Drake was playing boules as the Armada approached and famously said 'First we'll finish the game, then we'll deal with the Spanish'.*

Provence, in the south of France, and was known as *Jeu Provençal*. It involved a run up of a few paces before letting fly with the ball. *Pétanque* was born, rumour has it, when one of its greatest fans, Jules LeNoir, had an accident in 1910 and was confined to a wheelchair. As a result his friends changed the rules so that there was no run up and instead you played with your feet together – *pieds tanques* – which said with a southern accent sounds like 'pay tonk' or *pétanque*.

le cochonnet

There's not much to it – 12 *boules* made of steel (originally wood with loads of nails hammered in), a jack made of wood called *le cochonnet* (the piglet) and the aim is to get your boules closer to the piglet than your opponents. It can be played anywhere – rough, smooth, earth, sand or grass – and most importantly, like darts, it can be played with a glass in one hand.

Traditionally involving more drink than exercise, *pétanque* accessories include a magnetic lifter for those challenged by the effort required to pick up *les boules*. There may not be much physical exertion but there's always a lot of emotion in a game of *pétanque* – look out for the mutterings, grunts, rages, furrowed brows, yelps of joy and vigorous handshakes all round.

Le Tour de France

FRANCE'S NATIONAL obsession remains *Le Tour de France* – the greatest cycling endurance test in the world. The 2,500 mile route is known as *la Grande Boucle* – the big loop. It's been going for over a hundred years, takes 3 weeks in

July and ends in Paris usually around *Bastille Day* (14th July). Many books have been written on the rules and tactics of the Tour (yawn, yawn), so here's all you really need to know:

Jerseys (what all the fuss is about)

The Tour has 21 stages and whoever has the lowest time for all the previous stages put together gets to wear the all-important yellow jersey, *le maillot jaune.* So the overall winner is the person wearing the yellow jersey over the finishing line on the *Champs Elysée* (biggest street in Paris).

The last Frenchman to do this was Bernard Hinault in 1985. The French desperately need a new national hero to beat the record of the longest ever champion, Lance Armstrong, who is *(quel horreur)* American!

Then there are lots of points you can win along the way and

𝕳istorical 𝕹ote
In 1923 Pierre Labric cycled down all the stairs of the Eiffel Tower – incroyable!

the person with the most points gets to wear the green jersey – *le maillot vert*.

And then, and this is not for wimps, there's the King of the Mountains. Le Tour goes over the Alps and the Pyrenees and the cyclist who gets the most points over the summits gets to wear *le maillot à pois* – the jersey of peas – why it's called this is a bit of a mystery since it's actually white with red polka dots.

Tactics

One of the most important things is to pick the right moment for breaking away from the pack – the moment for having ants in the legs – *avoir des fourmis dans les jambes* – as they say. Sudden surprise bursts of acceleration can wrong-foot other competitors. The French even honour the most aggressive rider in the competition with a special number.

The packs do not consist of riders of equal status, like bees there are Queen bees and worker bees. The 'leaders' are surrounded by their *domestiques* – literally their servants. These cyclists are like motorbike outriders, they fetch water, they protect the leader from the wind and they pace him through the mountains.

The spectacle

Actually there's not much to see. The French get very excited when the Tour comes by and they all turn out to line the streets. First comes the Caravane Publicitaire which are all the sponsored floats. This carnival takes about an hour to go past and keeps the crowds amused before the cyclists flash past in a multi-coloured blurr (especially in flat areas where they're all cycling in a pack). Before you can tell your *maillot jaune* from your *maillot vert*, they're gone.

So keen are spectators to have a souvenir to show for all that hanging around, that fights routinely break out over discarded water bottles.

And remember: a *vélo* is a racing bike, never ever call it *une bicyclette* – that's what Monsieur Hulot rides.

Fin (The End)
Well done...

Fin (The End)

WELL DONE, YOU'VE finished the book and you can now pass yourself off as French!

If all's gone to plan and you've put in some practice, you should be throwing your hands around and kissing everyone in

English ado

sight. You've got your tongue and nose around *un bon vin blanc* and you've learnt *merde!* and *non!,* the two most important words in the French language. You've practised the gestures in the mirror and you're ready with *le bras d'honneur* at the passenger window.

You can match the French insult for insult but you also know how to flirt and chat them up.

You know how to steer clear of the more unappetising body parts on a French menu whilst you goggle at the body parts of the French rugby team. You can out-savvy a French waiter and walk with a baguette down your trouser leg.

You can piss in public with great aplomb and fart higher than your bum. You know how to address your family in *verlan* slang whilst you run the family car off plonk. You can behave like a French fashion designer whilst throwing balls at a piglet. You can discuss le zic and claim your rights.

France, watch out – here you come!

AND FINALLY, SOMETHING similar but this time using translations of some of the best French sayings:

You can show that you are not crazy the wasp (not born yesterday). *If someone is peeling your rush* (getting up your nose), *you can show you have nothing to polish* (don't give a damn), *be hard to cook* (put up a good resistance) *and, if necessary, nail the beak* (shut them up). *If you are in nice bed sheets* (in a fix) *or facing a bag of knots* (problem), *I have the flea at the ear* (suspect) *that for a blow of try, it will be a blow of master* (you'll make a good first attempt). *It is not the sea to drink* (not that difficult).

This book is not intended to look for the little beast (nitpick) *or swing a sluice* (have a dig) *at France. It may be cowly inflated* (have some cheek) *when it brushes a painting of* (describes) *the French but it is of good war* (fair's fair) *and it is of the same tobacco* (the same) *when the French brush a painting of* (describe) *the English. So please don't take the fly* (don't take offence).

The hope is that when you make yourself the suitcase (leave) *for France you will not have the bad of the country* (feel homesick), *you will discover that is has super owl living tongue* (a fantastic spoken language) *and it is cowly owl* (jolly nice). *In time you will learn to love your next* (neighbour).

But if you feel it makes white cabbage (failed completely) – *makes a duck* (hits the wrong note), *is a jerrican* (load of hot air) *or has made a stomach* (leaves you with egg on your face), *then you can always pull the hunt* (flush it) *down the little corner* (loo).

www.ingramcontent.com/pod-product-compliance
Ingram Content Group UK Ltd.
Pitfield, Milton Keynes, MK11 3LW, UK
UKHW041438180426
11947UKWH00007B/513